T0193884

Angels to Aliens

TRUE STORIES OF ENCOUNTERS WITH ENTITIES NOT OF THIS WORLD

Robert Ethier

authorHOUSE®

AuthorHouse™
1663 Liberty Drive
Bloomington, IN 47403
www.authorhouse.com
Phone: 1 (800) 839-8640

© 2019 Robert Ethier. All rights reserved.

No part of this book may be reproduced, stored in a retrieval system, or transmitted by any means without the written permission of the author.

Published by AuthorHouse 10/10/2019

ISBN: 978-1-7283-3133-1 (sc)
ISBN: 978-1-7283-3132-4 (e)

Library of Congress Control Number: 2019912803

Print information available on the last page.

Any people depicted in stock imagery provided by Getty Images are models, and such images are being used for illustrative purposes only. Certain stock imagery © Getty Images.

Scripture taken from The Holy Bible, King James Version. Public Domain

This book is printed on acid-free paper.

Because of the dynamic nature of the Internet, any web addresses or links contained in this book may have changed since publication and may no longer be valid. The views expressed in this work are solely those of the author and do not necessarily reflect the views of the publisher, and the publisher hereby disclaims any responsibility for them.

TABLE OF CONTENTS

PREFACE

I have personally interviewed all of the people who contributed stories for this book. I am convinced that what these people saw, heard, or felt actually happened to them. It is important to state that none of the people whose stories I share in this writing sought me out or wanted to tell their stories to the public. For that reason I will not disclose their identities or addresses.

The experiences with the paranormal described in this book are fascinating, frightening, and even horrifying. For some people who shared their stories, their experiences were enlightening and profound. During the process of researching and conducting interviews for *Angels to Aliens,* I have become a more spiritual person; I am grateful to those who shared their stories with me. I am also grateful to the investigators who spent hours with me in dark corners of basements and attics of homes in the hopes of encountering entities from another world.

I have been granted a peek into a world that exists not in the imagination, but in a reality that will cause you to question your own sanity. I wonder sometimes whether these creatures or beings visit us from another dimension, a parallel universe, or from another frequency in which our worlds make contact or mesh at the same time.

Regarding angels, I am convinced that their existence is for the enlightenment of our spirits and to assist us in our journey while we are here on this planet. It seems to me that angels are knowledgeable about the condition of a soul and the situation the soul seems to be experiencing at the moment of intervention. Angels purposely try to show their existence in a way that eases us of our burden if we ask for their help. I have heard that we are not human beings having a spiritual experience, but rather we are spiritual beings having a human experience here on Earth.

During my investigations and research I was not always able to differentiate a mischievous spirit from an evil one. Some cases still leave me feeling uneasy. It seems that some spirits intend to deceive their victims all along. That is, I believe that if a spirit or entity were once a human being of questionable character, a change of frequency or dimension would not alter that character defect.

Aliens seem to be the most troubling of all the entities and are completely out of most people's comfort zones. The fact they operate outside of the laws of the universe is understandable given they are superior and more advanced than we are. What terrifies me is that in the cases of abduction and interaction with humans, the people being taken and examined against their will cannot control what happens to them; they have to submit to the will of the captors. In some—if not all—reports of alien abductions, the abductees report being treated as if they were lower life forms, such as insects. The funny thing is that a lot of people who encounter these beings say the aliens look and move like insects themselves. Other people say they believe that aliens are Gods who created man in their image and wonder whether if that's the case, why abduct people and treat us as if meeting us for the first time?

Because I've spent so much time researching and listening to stories about these entities, I'm convinced that the world of the paranormal is as real as life and death but exists somewhere in between. I often wonder why some people have paranormal experiences and others do not.

If you've ever considered the possibility of an afterlife or encounters with beings from another dimension or aliens from outer space, I think you will enjoy this book. If you haven't, take my word for it. These true stories of such encounters will open your eyes to what is really out there.

ACKNOWLEDGMENTS

I would like to thank the people whose stories appear in this book for the time and energy they spent telling me about their experiences. You have all enlightened me about what we share this mysterious universe with, whether we like it or not. Amanda Grondin, artist and illustrator of the cover of this book for your insight, imagination and friendship. Matthew Underhill, for your technical support in keeping my ghost-hunting equipment and computer operating. Tim Weisberg, for inviting me on my first investigation with the gang. Matt Costa, Matt Moniz, and Mike Markowitz for sharing your experience with me. Readers of this book will appreciate all of your efforts.

Dedication To Linda, Adrienne, Michael, John, Shannon, Seth, Eric, Harbour, Calla, Chandler, Lisa, Dave, Sonya, Toni, Karen, Bill, Brian, Stefani, Tanner, Mia, Bobby, Jenn, and little Bobby, for your attendance at Uncle Bob's marshmallow pig roasts, where you allowed me to scare you to death with my ghosts stories. I loved every minute of it. You are my biggest fans.

Angelic Encounters

*Luke 22: 41-4.3. Then an angel appeared to him,
coming from heaven to give him strength."*

THERE GOES YOUR FATHER RIGHT THERE

Jacob's father was in a terrible battle for his life. He was hospitalized during the latter stages of cancer, confined to a bed in a hospital where his family lovingly prayed and cared for him for weeks. The nursing staff did all they could to make him comfortable during his last days here on Earth.

As is the case with many deaths, loved had to watch their family members suffering before the physical body succumbed to illness. Family members had enough time to say their goodbyes over the course of his hospitalization, but eventually his condition worsened and communication became impossible. Jacob's father became comatose at the end of his days. The family held a bedside vigil in shifts, as family members still had to work and keep their own families functioning as normal as possible.

Jacob was a farm operator and had to tend to such chores as feeding the animals and haying the fields. He was falling behind on his duties because of the situation. On the day his father passed away, Jacob had made arrangements with family members to work the farm. He had hoped to catch up some of the long overdue chores and return to the hospital that evening to sit with his Dad. That day the weather was warm and the sun was shining, a beautiful midsummer day with little or no wind.

Jacob was in the field cutting hay when he noticed a friend, his wife, and his son walking toward him. He got off the tractor and walked toward them. He said to himself, "this can't be good." He couldn't help noticing that off in a distance a small twister was forming. Jacob had not caught up to his visitors yet, but he could see that they were also watching the twister as it gathered speed. The tornado was gathering up loose pieces of hay that had been left on the field. It then sped toward Jacob as if on a predetermined course. When he told me this story he said, "It blew right through me." The twister collided with him, showering him with hay and debris and leaving him breathless. The twister then moved away slowly, eventually collapsing, spreading the debris it was carrying across the field.

After witnessing that amazing spectacle, Jacob's friend said, "There goes your father right now." He told Jacob they had come to tell him that his father had passed away.

THE HUNTING LICENSE

I have always been a spiritual person. Although I was raised Catholic, I haven't practiced my religion or attended church regularly. This story is absolutely true and really happened to me.

One evening during the fall of 2005, I was in my basement getting my gear together for a cool October evening of striped bass fishing. At the same time, I was gathering my hunting gear because the next day was the opening day of duck season on Cape Cod and I was hoping to bag a few ducks.

In the process, I remembered I had lost my hunting license a few months ago while in the woods tracking a wounded deer. I had looked unsuccessfully for the license many times over several months and had forgotten to replace it. I began calling family members, most of whom were not home at the time, to ask whether they had seen it. Everyone had been aware that it was missing for some time now and they all confirmed that they hadn't seen it.

My last hope was my oldest son, the only one home besides me, who was washing his car in the driveway. I asked him about the license as I had with the other family members. He replied, "You have been looking for that license for a long time and I'm pretty sure you're never going to find it."

I returned to the basement and sat down in front of my workbench to pray for divine intervention for the return of my license. I prayed, "God I need your help, I know, you know all about it, but I lost my license a number of months ago and I don't know what to do. I'm going fishing with a friend tonight and hunting with another friend in the morning before daylight and I don't have any more time to look for it, besides, I don't think it is here anyway. I am worried that I'll get caught without a permit or have my gun confiscated. I'm just worried that I would lose my gun and embarrass myself and my friend. Can you help me?"

I was sitting there for a minute or two when I heard the cellar door open. I turned around just in time to see my son throw the license down the cellar stairs. It landed on the floor. I ran outside and asked him, "Where did this come from?" He said, "A man walking his dog came up to me in the driveway and handed me the license. The man said, 'I just found this license, few blocks away lying in the street, and thought I'd bring it to you just in case you needed it.'"

Although we've lived in this neighborhood for many years, my son didn't recognize the person who delivered the license to the house in answer to my prayers that day. The license was in perfect condition with no signs of wear and tear or exposure to weather. I wonder where it had been all those months. I've thought about that incident many times and have told the story many more times than that. When people hear it, someone always asks whether it really happened. I always reply, "Absolutely!" I didn't add anything to the story that would make it more incredible than what it was. I always end the story by asking the listener, "What are the odds? They're astronomical."

A VISIT FROM SAINT NEKTARIOS

This story was told to me by a friend I will call Paul. Paul told me about an encounter his father had with a well-known monk in 1960. Paul's family lived in a small town called Salamis, on the Greek island of Aegina. Paul was 15 years old and was a member of a local Boy Scout troop. His family worshipped at a local parish whose tradition was to reenact the crucifixion of Jesus, beginning on Holy Thursday and culminating on Good Friday with a procession through the streets of their neighborhood. The parish priest, along with the parishioners, would nail a likeness of Jesus Christ to a cross on Holy Thursday. On Good Friday that likeness would be taken down and placed in a casket to be paraded through the town. Paul's scout troop customarily marched with the procession in the parade through the streets of Salamis. The parade would begin at the church, proceed through the streets, and eventually pass within a few hundred yards of Paul's family's house before ending at the church where the parade began.

On the morning of Good Friday, Paul asked his father for permission to march with the scout troop. His father gave Paul permission to walk from the church and through the town with the scouts, but when the parade reached his house Paul was to come home and not continue on to the church with the rest of the scouts. Paul was disappointed, but his disappointment was forgotten when he suddenly became ill. Because of the sudden onset and severity of Paul's illness, Paul's father called the local doctor to the home. Paul was given medication but it had little effect on him. He remained in bed and his father continued to check on him throughout the day. It was obvious that Paul would not march with his troop that afternoon.

Paul's father heard the procession as it passed near their home and he went outside to wave to the crowd. A monk approached and said, "Happy Easter, Mr. —," calling him by his last name. Paul's father returned to the house to find Paul standing in the bathroom washing his hands and face. Paul said, "I feel a lot better all of a sudden." His father was dumbfounded, trying hard to find an explanation for the sudden cure. He immediately ran back outside to find the monk, but the monk seemed to have vanished. This was strange because their house was located a couple hundred feet away from the road where the procession was traveling and one could see a person coming or going from a long way off in all directions.

After much reflection, Paul's father came to believe he was visited by St. Nektarios, the Monk that cured Paul of his affliction. Saint Nektarios died on November 8, 1920 and was canonized on April 20, 1961. Many miracles have been attributed to the saint, and many people have been visited by him, as Paul's father believes he was.

XXX/760

I was a diabetic for more than 20 years, and, having had enough of the complications of the disease, I asked my doctor whether I was eligible for a pancreas transplant. In 2005, I was interviewed and deemed eligible for the transplant at a local Boston hospital. There were a few requirements for eligibility. One was monthly tissue typing, which consisted of mailing a blood sample to a lab in Boston. Failure to follow these requirements could result in removal from the transplant list. Months passed, and I was beginning to experience complications from diabetes and poor blood sugar control. It was imperative that I have the transplant soon because I could not manage my diabetes very well.

After a particularly difficult day with fluctuating blood sugar levels, I realized I hadn't been to the lab for my monthly blood work. I was disappointed with myself for forgetting something so important, and that night I decided to have a chat with God. "God here's the deal," I began. "I am not feeling well more frequently now, and I don't think I can wait any longer for the transplant." I continued, "I don't think I could afford being out of work for however long the recovery time would be, I don't even know how long I've been on the list, so I think I'll take my chances the way I am." I fell asleep and woke in the middle of the night, recalling a dream in which I saw a sequence of numbers—a four-digit number and a three-digit number. I visualized the combination XXXX /760.

I went back to sleep and woke in the morning, paying little attention to the dream. About a week later, as I watched TV one evening the daily lottery numbers were announced. I noticed the four numbers were the same as those I'd seen in the dream. I hadn't played them and obviously I didn't win any money. However, I was convinced that if the four-number combination had won, the three-number combination 760 must be a sure thing. I played those numbers faithfully everyday for months.

On December 6, 2008, I got a call from the transplant center saying that a pancreas was available. I was told to get there that evening for surgery in the morning. On the way to the hospital I stopped at the store to play 760. However, that number never did win in any order. I have never played the numbers 760 again.

Months into my recovery, I got a call from the nurse coordinator to check on how I was feeling. At the end of the conversation, I asked, "How long was I on the transplant list?" I could hear typing on the keys of her computer, and after a short pause, she said "760 days."

MA

This is a story told to me by my Dad when he was gathered with his siblings at the bedside of his 88-year-old mother, who was dying of cancer. This woman had suffered many setbacks, trials, and tribulations in her life, and her belief in God and her Catholic religion was her salvation here on Earth. My grandmother was attended by hospice workers and loved ones who had watched her slip into a coma days before. My father called to update me on her condition and said that the hospice workers told the family that her condition was worsening rapidly and that she would expire within the next hour or so. Another call from my father verified that the hospice workers had been right; my grandmother did pass away. I asked my father "Did she say anything before she died?" He said, his mother said, "MA," blessed herself by making the sign of the cross and passed away.

YOU ARE GOING TO BE OK

Joe had just arrived at the medical center for what he thought was a routine check up on his heart when he learned that tests revealed a much more serious problem requiring emergency surgery. The doctor told Joe that open-heart surgery was imperative and that any delay may prove fatal. Joe was immediately prepped for surgery.

Joe told me that after being prepped for surgery, he was in a room waiting when he noticed a woman sitting in a chair next to him. She had on a big hat, and she looked very familiar— but Joe just couldn't place her. Joe finally got up the courage to ask her "Do I know you?" She replied, "You are going to be OK." Joe asked, "What are you doing here?" The woman replied, "Laureanne sent me." Laureanne was Joe's mother. Joe did make it through the surgery, just as the woman had told him he would. Joe told me he realized who the woman was— it was his mother's sister, a nun who lived in a convent for more than 50 years. Both sisters had passed away but were apparently watching over Joe even after death.

ANGELS IN THE CORNERS
OF THE ROOM

Todd's father was in the hospital and suffering from an illness that would eventually take his life. Todd said his father was beginning to see things that the rest of the family could not see. His father also spoke about people who came to visit him. "My father was not religious at all and I don't know if he believed in the afterlife," said Todd. "If he did he never spoke about it to his family."

As the illness progressed, His father became weaker, and he began speaking of visitors and angels he could see in the corners of the room near the ceiling. He eventually passed away. Todd believes his father was escorted to his destination into the afterlife by angels.

I UNDERSTAND YOU HAVE
SOME QUESTIONS FOR ME

Brian was 45 years old, married with four children, and he describes himself as a spiritual man. He had been raised Catholic but says he is not religious at all. Here is his story.

"Since I was a child I have always said my prayers before falling asleep. On this particular night, I was speaking with God about the sadness and pain that some people have to live through here on Earth. My family also has had some extremely difficult and sad events, the most devastating being the birth of our first child born with cerebral palsy and retardation as a result oxygen deprivation caused by a lack of proper medical care during delivery.

"Although I am quite sure God knows all about it, I still have questions about why things are the way they are and why they have to happen at all. When talking with others about the bad things that happen in this world I always say, 'When I get to heaven I am going to have a chat with God about that.' On this particular night while praying it dawned on me that when I do get to heaven and stand before God, I really wouldn't ask questions about unpleasant things on Earth. It also occurred to me that God was probably a little upset about my telling people about my plans for such a chat, as if I knew the reasons for anything. I apologized to God and promised him that I would never say that again.

"I fell asleep, and in a dream I woke to see the bedroom door open and a tall man enter the room. He stood facing me, as if he was waiting for something. He had long black hair and wore a light colored, full-length robe. I was not frightened at all. I don't know why, but I didn't look at him, and he didn't look at me, either. He seemed preoccupied with something else. I remember thinking of him as a sentry or guardian or something like that. Just seconds later, another man entered the room and walked past the guard who now was facing me. He, too, was dressed in a full-length robe. Still not frightened, I sat up and propped myself up with a pillow against the headboard of the bed. The second man moved toward the bed and sat down facing me. I remember thinking it was strange the way he sat down on the bed. He sat on his right side and turned to the right to look at me. Most people would have sat down on their left, as it was easier to look and talk to me directly. It just seemed awkward but didn't seem to bother him at all. I didn't say anything and he was the first to speak. He said, 'I understand you have some questions for me.' I said, 'Yes, I do.'

"I guess I knew all along that it was Jesus, but he didn't look like any of the pictures I had seen of him. I wasn't interested in his appearance, nor was I frightened or anxious. His demeanor was relaxing and he spoke softly. I began by asking Jesus about my daughter, specifically why she has to suffer so much. 'The answer to that question is this,' he said, and he gave me the answer. I remember asking, "Is it that simple, God?" I was dumbfounded but it was so simple that I understood it completely.

"He asked, 'What is your next question?' I asked him about the laws of nature and the universe, and again I was amazed at his answers. Jesus kept asking me whether I had other questions, and he kept answering each one as if we were talking about the weather or the scores of a sporting event.

"With each answer, I became increasingly amazed at how simple life really is. I realized that everything is in his plan and everyone has a plan. I kept repeating over and over as he answered each question for me, 'Is it that simple God? It can't be that simple.' The more information I was given the more excited I became. I remember experiencing a feeling of extreme wellbeing. I thought about death and dying in a whole new way. I was no longer afraid of the bad things that happen, because I knew that God knew all about it and it was okay.

"It may seem strange but in my dream Jesus didn't want to leave knowing I still had questions. At that time, I knew things that no one else knew and I felt no one would ever believe me if I tried to tell them what he told me. Somehow I knew that I wasn't going to pass this information on to anybody and this was between him and me. Jesus paused for a moment and said, 'Do you have any more questions for me?' It may seem strange but I replied, 'No I don't.' I raised myself up from the pillow, leaned closer to him, and I said, 'God, I promise, I will never question you again and I will tell everyone that you exist."

"Jesus nodded, stood up, turned toward the door, and walked out. The taller man then followed him out and shut the door behind them. I laid back down feeling exhausted and fell asleep almost instantly. I woke early the next morning and turned to look at the door, which was closed. I began to vividly recall my dream. I remembered the questions I asked but not the answers God gave me.

"I have recalled this dream and told my story to many people, and they all want to know what the answers were. I tell them that even though I don't remember the answers that doesn't mean there aren't any. I continue to nurture my relationship with God; I am never without council or direction.

"I had a friend who graduated from Harvard, who once asked me, 'If a genie appeared and gave you three wishes, would you use them?' I said, 'Of course I would.' He replied, 'You have something a million times more powerful than a genie, all you have to do is ask.'"

SECTION TWO

Ghostly Encounters

Luke 24.39. Touch me and make sure I am not a ghost, because ghosts don't have bodies, as you see that I do.

THERE IS SOMEONE OR SOMETHING
IN THIS HOUSE BESIDES US

During the late 1970s I built a house in a historical section of Buzzards Bay, Massachusetts. About one month after I moved in with my wife and three children, we began experiencing odd happenings inside the house. In the beginning, these occurrences were happening only at night.

The first experience took place at about 2 a.m., when my wife and I were awakened by the faint sound of music playing. It was hard to determine where the music was coming from. After some investigation, we found that the music was emanating from a music box in the closet in the master bedroom. The curious thing was that in order to activate the chime, someone would have to take it out of a box and open the drawer a certain distance. Since the box was exactly the same size as the jewelry box, it was impossible to open the drawer at all. This incident repeated a number of times, until I finally removed the drawer. Only then did the music stop playing.

A few months later, my oldest son, who was 8 at the time, began talking about an imaginary friend he called Autie. My son spoke of Autie from time to time, and on one occasion he looked out the living room window and said, "Look, Autie is in the grass." My wife and I looked out the window but we couldn't see what he was calling Autie. We asked him why we didn't see him even though he was convinced Autie was there. That was the only time we know of that my son saw Autie outside the house. This was interesting because as the occurrences continued and the phenomenon increased, more strange activity involving children presented itself.

By this time it was apparent to my wife and I that something or someone had manifest itself in our house and was becoming increasingly aggressive. Whatever was causing the disturbances in the house now focused on the windows instead of the music box. It seemed to me that while turning on the musical jewelry box in the middle of the night was playful and harmless, slamming the windows seemed aggressive and, because of the loud noise, more frightening.

Summer came, and since we didn't have air conditioning in the house we kept most of the windows open day and night. We built the house using top-of-the-line materials, including the windows that were easily opened and closed. The windows were equipped with latches to hold the windows open in several positions to control air circulation on a particular day. All windows had locks on both sides, and if a lock were not engaged properly on one side of the window the other lock would keep the window from shutting accidently.

To my recollection, shortly after the music box incidents windows began to slam shut at odd moments. This didn't happen every night, and not all windows were involved. It was now obvious that whatever was slamming the windows was doing this intentionally and with malice. I can remember one occasion that three windows slammed shut at different times on the same night. The windows involved were in the kitchen, the living room, and in our boys' bedroom. Curiously, these were also the rooms in which we had already experienced strange activity. If I was home and heard a window slam I would immediately seek out the source of the noise, and almost every time I would find that window closed. I began to wonder whether the window had been closed all along and was opened and slammed shut to get our attention. I guess I wanted to believe that the windows were defective and there was nothing sinister was responsible for the incidents. However, I suspected that maybe the slamming was directed by an unknown entity without ever touching the windows at all. At no time was anyone in the house or room to witness the window slamming.

As these incidents continued, they became more baffling to me. I avoided mentioning them to my wife because I didn't want to frighten her. The more I tried to figure out what was happening, the more unusual the events became. As these unexplained phenomena continued, my wife and I began rationalizing them. However, no matter how we tried to explain away the odd happenings, they continued.

During one period, we heard loud bangs mostly in the early evening at the rear of the house. The noise sounded as if someone was hitting the house with a sledgehammer or rock. When I heard the noise I'd rush outside to try to catch someone in the act. I inspected the siding but I never saw any visible marks or damage on the siding.

Just as the playing of the music box and the slamming windows had continued for a couple of weeks and ceased completely, the banging eventually stopped. I was relieved as my son spoke less and less about his invisible friend Autie. Looking back, although this was very strange I did not relate the imaginary friend with the seemingly more aggressive happenings in the house. After the window banging stopped, I had no more rationalizations. I became convinced that there was a presence in the house. Every time I left the house at night I felt uneasy that my family was alone with whatever it was.

A few weeks later, banging noises began in the unfinished downstairs basement. I began to wonder whether the banging that occurred at the back of the house hadn't actually come from the basement the whole time. However, the sounds were different. Unlike the single loud blows that we heard from outside the house, the new sounds were a series of constant muffled banging interrupted by an occasional loud bang. I would sit at the top of the stairs leading down to the cellar of the split-level home and wonder what the hell was down there. At no time were the noises that began in the basement ever as loud as those we heard striking the house from outside or the slamming of the windows.

The muffled banging would quiet for a few days then begin again with more intensity. I'm convinced that when we got comfortable in the house again after an episode, the entity would become angry with us and begin a new assault. I was growing increasingly despondent and frightened because I felt that the entity knew that I sensed it was there. I swear that if I deliberately ignored it, the basement noises would become so loud and fast that no one could ignore it. I tried to compare the sound of the heating system from the banging noises and there was no comparison. At times it seemed as if someone or something was taping on the walls and other times, it seemed as if the tapping was on the steel columns down there. The entity now concentrated on the downstairs. I remember feeling relieved that it wasn't upstairs anymore, and I avoided the basement at night.

My son with the imaginary friend happened to be sick one night with a slight fever. We gave him some children's aspirin and put him to bed. Later we heard him giggling in his room. I went to see what he was laughing about. "There are little kids playing in the hall and they want me to play with them," he said. We attributed the incident to his elevated temperature and dismissed it. However, a couple of weeks later I was awakened at about 2 a.m. by what appeared to be children playing in the kitchen.

I recall an overcast night with no moon visible, making it completely dark in the kitchen. This was a split-level house with a kitchen, dining room, bathroom and three bedrooms on the main floor. You could exit the master bedroom into the hallway, look to the left and see my daughter's bedroom. Straight ahead but to the right was the bathroom, and to the immediate right of the master bedroom, off the hallway, was the boys' bedroom. The kitchen was at the end of the hall about 12 feet from the doorway of the master bedroom and 6 feet from the doorway of the boys' bedroom. I lay in bed listening, sure it was my boys playing in the kitchen with toy cars. My wife had also awakened. "Do you believe this?" she said. "The boys are playing with cars in the kitchen and it's completely dark in there!" Looking out into the hallway I saw nothing but total darkness.

We both heard two children, maybe more, running a matchbox car across the linoleum floor in the kitchen. The cars sounded like the ones that a child rolled backward and were held in place before they'd propel themselves forward across a flat surface. Someone or something was revving up the cars and propelling them across the floor. We could actually hear the cars hit the wall. I also heard footsteps of children running across the floor to fetch the cars and return to propel them against the wall—back and forth, back and forth. I listened for a couple of minutes, but it seemed like forever. Finally my wife asked, "Are you awake? Can you believe the boys are playing with cars in the kitchen?"

I was relieved that she was hearing what I was, but I immediately felt sick to my stomach because I knew that what we thought we heard couldn't really be happening. The boys wouldn't be up playing at this time of the night, especially in total darkness. The kitchen activity continued as my wife and I whispered to each other. I believe the entity could hear us too. I jumped up on the bed and, using the bed as a springboard, leapt into the hallway. The noises stopped. I turned on the hall light and peered into the now semi-darkness of the kitchen. I strained to see into the shadows for the source of the noise. It took a few seconds to gather my wits about me as I made my way toward the kitchen trying to find the light switch. As I did, I desperately searched for evidence that would verify what we had been hearing. I found the switch and turned it on. There were no cars or toys of any kind on the floor, tables or counters.

From the hall I could see that all of the children were sound asleep in their rooms. I returned to the bedroom and sat up in bed wondering what had just happened. Although this event hadn't been as aggressive as the other phenomena, I was sure that whatever was responsible for the noises was aware we heard them, just as I was aware they heard us. I believe the kitchen noises were another attempt by whatever was in the house to get our attention. The noises stopped immediately after I appeared in the hallway and that was the end of it. We never again heard or experienced noises in the kitchen or elsewhere in the house. We lived in the house 16 more years, and my son never talked about his friend Autie during that time.

While the strange phenomena were going on, I noticed there was always a time of inactivity between events. It seemed the entity was either resting to build up energy or thinking of new ways to frighten us. It was almost as if it waited for us to drop our guard before resuming the strange activity. Truthfully, I was never comfortable living in that house since the first incidents took place. What's more, I was never thrilled about leaving my family alone in the house at any time of day.

After we lived in the house for about a year, things quieted down with the exception of some banging in the basement. We hired a contractor to finish the basement with plans for a family room, spare bedroom, and laundry room. There was a closet under the stairs and a small workshop area with a coal stove to supplement the expensive electric heating. There was also a garage large enough for one car with some storage. Over the next few months, banging and other unidentifiable noises began with more fervor and aggressiveness than ever. Meanwhile, upstairs, activities proving to be even more baffling—and expensive—resumed.

One day the following spring my wife casually asked me whether I'd seen one of her watches. She said she had assumed that she had taken it off a few days before to wash dishes but now it was missing. We both figured that she'd simply misplaced the watch and it would turn up someplace soon. A couple weeks later, she asked if I had seen her other watch, which was now missing as well. Over the years I had bought her jewelry for birthdays and anniversaries and she had accumulated quite a lot. Now it seemed to be disappearing, one piece at a time.

My wife kept her jewelry in a stand-up jewelry box, still in there original boxes. Unless the boxes were opened, she couldn't tell that something was missing. The jewelry box was in the master bedroom about six feet from the closet where the smaller musical jewelry box had been waking us up months before. By this time we had lost only two watches, and my wife checked all the other boxes and found everything there. Naturally, I checked all windows and doors, found the house to be secure, and therefore found no reason to believe someone was entering the house and stealing her jewelry. However, jewelry pieces continued to disappear every two or three weeks until they were gone. We called the police and filed an insurance claim. The jewelry was never recovered.

Later, after the entity remained quiet for a while, we heard banging and knocking noises in the now-finished basement. At first, the noise was subtle, but as the weeks passed the banging increased in volume and urgency. It was hard to ignore, as the banging continued to the point that it I was constantly aware of it. I began to have trouble sleeping, and when I did fall asleep I started having violent nightmares. I decided that ignoring the events was the worst the thing to do.

One night I was home alone when the activity in the basement had become so loud it seemed to be challenging me to confront it. It was nighttime, and for some reason I wanted to confront it myself. I didn't want to turn on the basement lights and make it disappear as it had in the past, so I grabbed a flashlight from the kitchen and started down the eight or nine steps from the foyer to the basement. As I negotiated the last step, the noises seemed to escalate as if the thing was excited to finally get the chance to confront me. I somehow summoned the courage to yell, "If the devil is in the cellar prove it to me now!" With a pop, the bulb in my flashlight blew out. I stood frozen with fear on the last step feeling as if my legs would collapse. I don't remember how long I stood there before it occurred to me that the noises had stopped. Everything was deathly quiet. I strained to listen for the entity coming after me then ran back up the stairs.

Back in the kitchen I prayed to God to protect my family and then called a Catholic priest. The priest, a friend of mine, agreed to perform a blessing the following weekend. I told my wife that I would meet the priest alone. In the meantime, I avoided the basement. Waiting for the priest was the hardest thing I've ever done. The house was quieter than it had been for a long time, and every night I lay in bed wondering whether the entity was resting in wait for the priest's arrival. Sunday finally came and after I greeted the priest, he immediately began the task of blessing the house. I followed him around room by room waiting for a sign of the entity's presence and wondering whether it was going to make itself known to the priest as it had to me. The priest seemed hesitant at times and I wondered whether he was sensing something in the house.

After the blessing was completed, we had a lunch my wife had prepared, I thanked him for his services, and he left. I was in the house alone for a few hours alone before my family returned and I spent most of that time wondering if I could drop my guard. The house didn't seem different in any way—probably because I wasn't sure whether I could let myself relax enough to feel the difference.

I never told my wife what I experienced on the stairs the night the flashlight bulb blew out, nor did I tell the priest about anything that had happened in the house. In fact, I never discussed anything we experienced to anyone for fear of ridicule. After moving into that house in Buzzards Bay the paranormal activity plagued us for about two years. After the blessing, we continued to live there uneventfully for another 16 years. We sold the home in 1998 to a retired couple and built another one in the same neighborhood. We have never again been bothered by music boxes, children playing with cars at night, or things that go bump in the basement.

I THINK THERE IS
SOMETHING UPSTAIRS

In 2009, CJ and Jennifer moved into a relatively new house in Monument Beach, Massachusetts, with their three sons. Almost immediately, it became apparent to CJ that the house was extremely noisy, and he mentioned to Jennifer about noises that seemed to be coming from upstairs. CJ remembers that on the family's first night in the house, Jennifer wanted to bring their nine-year-old son into their room to sleep on the floor because the noises were so loud he would be frightened.

Most of the family slept upstairs. But the son, who was 14, had a room downstairs. When I spoke to CJ, he said, "The house was noisy from the first day we moved into it. There were constant noises coming from inside the walls of the house." CJ added that the strangest and most memorable noise was faint, rapid knocking as if a visitor was becoming impatient for someone to answer the door. At first, CJ said, he thought the noises were due construction or settlement issues but it soon became apparent that wasn't the case with this house.

After the family had moved in, CJ and his father had remodeled the pantry, adding some shelves for storing groceries and canned goods. Eventually, it became clear that the pantry had become a hotspot of paranormal activity. No one seemed comfortable there. If someone needed something from the pantry, he or she would run in, grab what was needed, and beat a hasty retreat.

Shortly after settling in the house, Jennifer and CJ were sound asleep when at about 2 a.m., the bathroom door slammed open with such force that it woke them both. The force caused the door to wedge itself against the bathtub, requiring a crowbar to free it. At night the couple usually left the door open so they could hear the children. Jennifer seemed to know exactly where the noise had come—the bathroom door. CJ jumped from the bed, grabbed a golf club, and began searching the house for an intruder. Jennifer said that CJ returned from the search and sat on the edge of the bed shivering uncontrollably. She explained that she was frightened by his demeanor and asked repeatedly what he saw. CJ didn't look at her as he sat on the edge of the bed with his back to her. She said, "CJ told me he didn't want to talk about it."

Eventually CJ climbed into bed but he couldn't stop shivering until he was under the blankets for a while. After interviewing the both of them regarding that incident, I decided that CJ and Jennifer had totally different memories about how long CJ had been downstairs. CJ thought that he was gone from the room for five minutes or so but Jennifer stated that he was actually downstairs for at least 20 minutes or more. CJ said he doesn't remember what he encountered that night and doesn't even remember descending the staircase looking for whomever or whatever had slammed the bedroom door with such force.

There were times when the couple would find their two-year-old son staring at something and other times they would hear him laughing at whatever he appeared to be seeing. The strange happenings were not limited to CJ, Jennifer, and their youngest son; their 10-year-old son began talking about a seeing a small boy walk by the door to his room, up the stairs, and out of sight. According to CJ, that was the only time a member of the family saw an apparition in the home but not the last time they would experience paranormal activity in the house.

CJ and Jennifer related another incident that happened to them in the kitchen one evening. CJ said, "We were having a glass of wine together. Our two-year-old son was playing with his toys in the adjoining room when I heard him giggling. We walked into the room but couldn't see him at first. We scanned the room and started to call his name and found him perched on a cabinet against the wall. The cabinet was about four feet off the floor, and there was no way he could have climbed to the top of that shelf by himself. Someone would have had to pick him up and place him there. We never spoke about that incident again but we both were nervous about taking our eyes off him again. He too fair game for our invisible intruder."

CJ described a different night that he was home alone, with Jennifer out of town attending a wedding. He was having trouble sleeping and decided to get a bottle of water. CJ walked downstairs into the pantry and reached for the bottle. He said, "I felt as if someone was standing very close behind me, and the hair on the back of my neck began to rise. I heard someone whisper *CJ* into my ear. It sounded like the scratchy and weak voice of an older woman."

"Although very frightened, I became angry and yelled at the invisible intruder, 'You'd better leave my family alone! If you hurt anybody in this house I will burn it down. I swear I will do it!'"

CJ told me he walked back up to the bedroom and lay down on the bed with youngest son when suddenly the bed they were sleeping in crashed to the floor. CJ said, "It felt as if a three hundred pound man had jumped from the ceiling onto the bed." The boards on the bottom of the bed frame were broken from the force of whatever it was. CJ couldn't get back to sleep that night although things remained quiet. CJ kept most of his experiences with the intruders to himself to avoid frightening his wife any more than she was. He said that didn't know whether the entity would heed his warning to leave his family alone.

Shortly after that episode, Jennifer had a frightening mishap while driving with their two youngest children in the car. The car was brand new, making the mishap that day even more baffling. As on any typical workday morning, Jennifer was on her way to drop off the children at the sitter's house and school when the car appeared to shut down. Instantly, Jennifer lost all control of the vehicle as it pulled to the right and almost off the road. Somehow she managed to get the vehicle back under control and drive it slowly to the dealership.

Mechanics at the dealership were unable to diagnose the problem and the car had to be sent to another dealership, where it was eventually repaired. The repairs were expensive, and the experts who worked on the vehicle couldn't explain what caused the malfunction. During the repair process, CJ traded vehicles with Jennifer. Although she didn't experience any serious breakdowns with CJ's car while she used it, the alternator died and needed to be replaced.

At this time, CJ was becoming more and more angry and despondent toward Jennifer and their relationship was beginning to fall apart. CJ couldn't explain the anger he was experiencing and had resorted to sleeping on the living room couch downstairs. One evening, CJ had just turned off the television and turned over to go to sleep when he heard the TV come back on. He opened his eyes to see that, in fact, the television was back on. CJ placed the remotes on the table in front of him and said, "Do that again." Seconds later, the lights on the remotes lit up and the television turned on again. CJ told me he went upstairs and crawled into bed next to his wife. At this point he knew that not only was there something in the house but it was now interacting with him and obviously could manipulate electronic devices on command. CJ was convinced that the entity understood what he was saying. It had his attention!

As the strange activity increased, the couple's relationship was falling apart. So CJ decided to leave the house and find another place to live. Jennifer tried to carry on with her responsibilities, such as work and being a mother to her children. She told me that she really had not experienced what CJ had. "To be honest," she told me, "I really don't believe in ghosts or the paranormal."

A few weeks later, Jennifer was awakened by the sensation of someone applying pressure to her chest. She said, "I woke up gasping for breath, and the pain in my chest was excruciating." She added, "When I recovered and caught my breath, I called CJ in a panic, crying about what had just happened to me. He came over as fast as he could." CJ told me that after comforting Jennifer, he fell asleep and had a horrible dream. 'I was dreaming that I was in a room with old-fashioned décor and there I saw a woman bathing herself in a copper tub. She had her back toward me and was splashing water over her back. I kept staring at her and it seemed to me that she knew that I was watching her. As I glanced around the room at the furnishings to help me understand what it was that I was seeing, I noticed an old antique full-size dressing mirror exactly opposite the woman in the tub. I focused on the image in the mirror I was terrified to see an old hag with absolutely horrifying features who looked more like a corpse that had been dead for a while. It took a while to get the dream out of my head and I could not get back to sleep that night. Things always seem less scary in the day light hours but I could not stop thinking about the dream or what had tried to harm Jennifer that night. We knew now that whatever was sharing space with us in that house was not friendly and that it was no longer content with just knocking on walls and playing with the remote controls."

Jennifer told me that CJ left after the incident that morning and remained living in an apartment by himself and added that he was always there when she called for support in dealing with her invisible intruder. The horrifying events of that evening were to be repeated two more times. The second incident was basically the same as the first, with the entity trying to squeeze the breath out of her, resulting in intense pain. Jennifer said that during the third incident she was again awakened, and while gasping for breath she saw a black mist hovering above her body. As she lay there horrified, she watched it move to the opposite side of the bed where CJ slept. It hovered above the pillow on that side of the bed before vanishing completely.

After witnessing the mist and feeling that the attacks were becoming much more sinister, Jennifer feared for her life and the wellbeing of her family. Although more time remained on the lease, she left that house that day. CJ returned with family members to retrieve their belongings. Jennifer has met the new tenants of the Monument Beach house but for fear of ridicule is reluctant to ask whether they are experiencing anything unusual. Jennifer and CJ continue to live separate lives, and it appears that as of the writing of this story, the entity has not followed either one of them to new residences.

ROGER'S STORY

Roger and I had been friends for a long time when he purchased an old home in a small Cape town. The house had a particularly gruesome past, and because of that history I talked about it with Roger before and after the purchase. Roger knew the former owner and his family and was aware that the owner and a member of his family had committed suicide on the property at different times.

Despite my concerns and warnings, Roger strenuously denied any belief in the paranormal. I told him I was concerned that there might have been an evil presence in the house that drove the two people to suicide. Roger wasn't interested in my theories and went about the business of moving his family into the two-story colonial home. The family painted walls, replaced old flooring and carpeting and remodeled the kitchen.

The family seemed comfortable with their new home. A couple of months later, however, they began experiencing occasional strange and unusual happenings. Roger seemed embarrassed at first to mention what was happening because of his earlier insistence that he had never witnessed anything paranormal and did not believe anything existed after death.

Even when strange things started to happen in the house, Roger wasn't afraid, as most people who knew the house's history would be. However, I could hear a sense of confusion in his voice one day when he told me what he'd witnessed a couple of nights previous. It was a couple of weeks before Christmas and we were having dinner at a restaurant. Roger shook his head and said, "Bob, what I'm going to tell you is messed up." He recalled that as he sat reading in his recliner near the Christmas tree, a gust of wind blew from behind the Christmas tree toward him. The wind was strong enough to blow the tinsel on the branches straight out. It was a sustained wind that lasted for 15 or 20 seconds and made a whistling noise as it blew through the tree. Roger said he checked the front door, which was closed and locked. It was a cold night but there was no wind. The room is in the middle of the house, and a hallway would have blocked any wind from the front door had it been open. The conversation changed to sports and politics and we didn't speak of the incident again.

The holidays came and went, and sometime in early January or late February, Roger and I got together again. I was curious about whether he had experienced anything out of the ordinary and asked, "How's the house?" Roger paused for a minute, took a deep breath, and said, "I know you are going to think I am crazy, but listen to this." He continued to explain that the family had just purchased a big screen television set. Roger was again reading a book in the living room and heard a voice coming from the television set.

"The voice said, 'Hi, Roger.' I was sure I heard the voice talking to me and I was sure it was coming from the new television set but it was not turned on at the time." Now I could sense the fear that Roger felt, and I could tell it was causing him a lot of anxiety. To be honest with you I was scared for him too. From Roger's description, I got the impression that the voice was trying to scare him and not just casually saying 'hello.'

At Roger's request, I took some photographs and checked the house out one night but I didn't pick up anything out of the ordinary. I wanted to bring in a team of investigators, which included a couple of psychics, but worried that I would make things worse for Roger and his family. I did provide him with some holy water, but I don't know if he ever used it.

I met up with Roger and his wife some weeks later and asked, again, "How's the house?" He replied, "Ask my wife. She had an encounter in the upstairs bedroom with an unseen force that was not happy with her."

Roger's wife, Darlene, said, "I was reading in the upstairs bedroom when something caught my attention. I looked at the nightstand and saw a tube of my lipstick lift straight up off the stand, fly across the room, hit the wall, and shatter into pieces." She said she ran downstairs to tell Roger. The woman spoke as if she already knew the family was sharing the house something that at the very least knew their names and could interact with them.

Roger and Darlene sold the house shortly afterward, and although Roger told me he would ask the new owners if they every experienced anything unusual in the house, I don't think he did. Roger died of cancer sometime after selling that house, and the new owners haven't disclosed whether they are experiencing the same paranormal activity.

A MURDER OF CROWS

S tephen was a director at an assisted living community in the southeastern part of Massachusetts. He has personally experienced numerous accounts of paranormal activity within the building and on the property. Residents and support staff have reported nightly visits from ghost children, who appear to be playing in a world of their own, oblivious to the residents. The residents claim that they can see and hear the children playing and running through the halls of the facility. The reports are similar among different residents, who report seeing the same number of children performing the same activities. More than one resident has reported seeing apparitions coming from a trap door that mysteriously appears in the floor of a couple of rooms.

Stephen told me that a woman who worked the evening shift continually complained about a murder of crows that started at her through her windows at night and sometimes follow her to work.

Stephen said, "She worked as an aide on the overnight shift, and I didn't believe what she told me. I watched her perform a ritual of closing curtains on more than one occasion. She would become more and more anxious as nighttime approached. I dismissed her behavior as a fear of the dark, and thought to myself that maybe something traumatic had happened to her in the past that caused her fear.

"Early one morning I was summoned to the facility because of a problem that needed my immediate attention. As I drove into the parking lot, I noticed her car. What I saw made the hair stand up on the back of my neck. Out of all the cars in the parking lot, only her car was surrounded by crows. The birds were standing on the roof and hood of the car. Some were walking around the vehicle while others stood still on the pavement around the car. The birds didn't seem interested in any other vehicles, just hers. They didn't make a sound, and it was as if they were waiting for the woman to come out. I didn't see her leave the building that morning, at the end of her shift, but I often wondered how she reacted to the crows waiting for her in the daylight She quit her job sometime after that incident, and I have not seen the crows in the parking lot or on the property again."

WHAT THE HELL WAS THAT?

During the 1990s, I myself actually witnessed the results of unexplained events that took place in a house in Buzzards Bay Massachusetts. My brother-in-law was renting a home and he and my sister in law were experiencing the beginnings of what seemed like a haunting. The couple would call me and relate stories of strange things that would take place, such as objects changing location and, on more than one occasion, the apparition of a girl's reflection in the bathroom mirror. From my kitchen window, I could clearly see their basement windows, and sometimes at night I could see the basement lights going on and off presumably by themselves.

My brother-in-law had a reputation as a prankster, and the family wasn't sure if he was kidding. The couple lived in the house for some time, and they spoke less about events taking place in the home as time went by. Eventually, they became more relaxed living there. However, one night that feeling was shattered by fear and the realization that whatever shared the house with them was angry and took it out on the furniture.

Early one morning I received a call from my brother-in-law, who said something frightening had happened the previous night. He described what they thought was an explosion in the house that woke everybody and scared them so badly that they hardly slept the rest of the night. The sound sent him running through the house looking for the cause of the noise. He and his wife worried that their daughter had fallen down the stairs, but she had not. The search continued. The last place they searched was the master bedroom. Opening the closet door, the couple was immediately overcome by astonishment and fear at what he saw.

The next day, we discussed the incident over the phone. I promised to meet the couple at the house after work to see for myself the results of the previous nights' events. When I arrived, I found them huddled on the front step of the house. It was clear they had not yet entered the house and were still extremely anxious about what had happened the night before. They both requested that I bring some holy water and perform a blessing before either would stay in the house that night. I entered the house with my brother-in-law, but my sister-in-law stayed outside on the step.

The events of the previous night still on her mind, even though it was dark outside, my sister-in-law felt more comfortable outside the house than inside. I began blessing the rooms, making my way to the master bedroom. Upon entering the room, I sprinkled the holy water around and opened the closet door. To my amazement, most of the boards in the closet, such as the pole, shelf, and the two-by-four brackets holding the shelf in place were in pieces on the floor of the closet. It was as if something with enormous strength had grabbed both sides of the shelf and snapped it in half. Some of the pieces of wood looked as if they were twisted as they were being broken, leaving the ends splintered and shredded. I couldn't explain what had happened to them that night, and I could find no signs of similar damage anywhere else in the house. The couple never took any pictures, and they moved soon after that incident. There have relocated and report no further incidents of paranormal activity.

FUNERAL PARLOR GUEST

I interviewed a funeral director named Paul about an experience he had while working as an apprentice in Jamaica Plain, Massachusetts, in 2001. Because of his training and education, Paul had never entertained any ideas that life existed after a person died. However, Paul told me about an experience that made him reconsider his beliefs.

"It was a Saturday morning and I was working alone and had just finished embalming a client," Paul explained. "All of a sudden my dog, Mike, who accompanied me whenever I was alone or worked during the weekends, began barking in the direction of the corpse on the table. He nudged me out of the way and positioned himself between the corpse and me, continuing to bark and to posture aggressively toward an invisible intruder near the corpse. This continued for a while, his behavior becoming increasingly aggressive. So I decided to grab him and leave the building immediately. I literally had to drag him away from that room. This took me by surprise and made me feel very uncomfortable. My dog had accompanied me several times to that location but had never reacted like that before and has not since. I wonder sometimes what would have happened to me if my dog were not there to protect me. I am now a funeral director, with a business of my own, and I have never witnessed anything like that again. I hope I never do."

THE HOUSE THAT GOT EVEN

T his incident took place in a small southeastern farming town settled originally by Quakers, descendants of the pilgrims. James was on duty as a call firefighter one evening when a call came into the station that a remote alarm detected smoke at an unoccupied residence.

The duty crew responded to the scene and verified that no fire or smoke was evident inside or outside the house. The house was scheduled to be torn down by the heirs and there was construction equipment and dumpsters on site. About 20 minutes later, as the crew was preparing to return to the station, fire dispatch notified the crew that a smoke alarm was again activated at the residence.

The crew entered the house a second time. James detected smoke in the den on the first floor and a smell that indicated something was on fire in the room. Upon further investigation, James noticed a picture on the wall aflame but the fire went out as mysteriously as it had begun. James noticed that the fire appeared to have started halfway up the frame and burned to the top of the picture and frame. The bottom half had not been touched at all by fire. Neither the picture nor the wall behind it was hot to the touch. No one could identify the image inside the frame.

I asked James whether the frame was recovered for evidence or further examination, and he stated it was not. James and the rest of the firemen continued to the second floor to look for other sources of the smoke. While ascending the stairs, he felt as if he was engulfed in a pocket of cold air. James called out to the other firemen, saying that the air conditioning was on upstairs.

According to James, it was a hot and humid night, and the cold air was noticeable. Once the firemen got to the second floor, they realized that the cold air was restricted to the stairway. They crew knew there had been no electrical power to the house since the last resident was moved to a nursing home.

As a joke, the crew assigned a recruit to stay the night at the house alone to stand fire watch. The recruit had been making negative comments about the house being haunted and the weird events of the evening. They eventually told him that they were just kidding with him. When the crew was satisfied that another alarm was unlikely, they returned to the station and the call firemen returned to their homes and jobs. The recruit returned to his job at a marina.

That evening the fire department was dispatched to a local marina for a vehicle fire. They arrived at the scene to discover that the burning vehicle was owned by the recruit who had made negative comments about the abandoned residence that they had responded to earlier that day.

THE INDIAN ON THE WATER

About fifteen years ago, a friend and colleague told me an interesting story about an apparition that his wife saw at Lake Nippenicket in Bridgewater, Massachusetts. He said, "My wife works as a nurse at a local medical facility and she usually takes the same route home every night. One of the roads she travels takes her on Route 104, which runs east to west and at one point takes you past Lake Nippenicket, locally called 'the Nip.' It was dark at the time and as she passed the Nip something caught her eye. She said she saw an Indian standing on the water wearing a full headdress. A bright golden light surrounded his silhouette."

I've told this story a few times to locals who told me that there have been many stories of Indians standing on or canoeing on the lake, and that they, too, are surrounded in a brilliant light.

Lake Nippenicket

THANKS FOR STOPPING BY

A young man named Jack who was visiting a friend and a relative buried in a cemetery on Shore Road in Monument Beach, Massachusetts, told this story to me. Jack made it a point to stop at the gravesites when in the area to pay his respects. After stopping at the site of his friend's grave, Jack stopped at the site of his grandmother who had passed on some years before. It had been years since he had been at the grave. Jack said he spoke to his grandmother and said the things that one would when visiting someone who has moved on. Jack told me his grandmother was born in Germany. She spoke with an accent and as she grew older it was more pronounced. Jack said he left the cemetery that day and promised to stop by again when in the area.

Weeks later, Jack said he was contracted to install and connect cable to a television set for a woman who happened to be a medium and whose claim to fame was conversing with the dead. After completing the installation, the woman approached Jack and told him that she had been given a message for him from someone who had passed on. The woman said the person spoke with an accent and was hard to understand. However, the message was "Thanks for stopping by the other day."

FORT KNOX ANOMALY

In June of 2013, Karen and Bill visited the Fort Knox historic site in Prospect Maine. They wandered around the fort taking photographs, hoping to capture something unusual on film. They had both heard rumors of the fort being haunted, so they thought they would do some investigating on their own. They went to the officers quarters, were it has been rumored that a soldier appears, mostly to women, Bill was in another part of the officers quarters next door. Karen said, "I thought I would see if I could get something to appear to me alone. I began to speak to whatever was in the room by asking, "If there is anyone in here, please show yourself to me" Karen then started taking pictures.

"Bill walked into the room immediately afterward. We looked at the camera screen and couldn't believe what we saw. The photo taken after my request to the resident ghost showed some kind of a spiraling smoke or light along with numerous orbs. Neither one of us had ever seen anything like that before. We took other pictures, but nether the strange smoke or the orbs appeared in any other photo."

First photo

Second photo

CEMETERY ORB

It was overcast day in early fall, about an hour before sunset, and I was on the way to meet my team of researchers to investigate a supposed haunted house. I noticed a cemetery on the side of the road. I was a little early so I decided to stop and take a couple of photographs to see if I could pick up anything unusual on film.

As I walked up the hill to the cemetery from the side of the road, I was immediately struck by the peacefulness of the place. The headstones were old and the ground around the graves was littered with broken branches and leaves. It was eerily quiet and cool with no breeze. I saw nothing unusual in the graveyard and began taking pictures. After snapping eight pictures I returned to my vehicle and drove away to meet my friends. Later, I downloaded the pictures to my computer and that's when I noticed an orb, about the size of a softball, which seemed to be suspended about two to three feet above the ground. No other anomalies were visible in any of the other photographs.

Cemetery orb

THE CAT THAT WOULDN'T LEAVE

This story was told to me by relatives who lost their beloved cat TC in 2007. He was a handsome cat, black with white paws, with a personality of his own. The family of four enjoyed him from the time they got him as a kitten to the end of his days, which totaled eighteen years. About two weeks after his passing, family members began swapping stories about experiences they were having, such as hearing a cat purring in their ears while sleeping.

"It is hard to say who TC came to visit first because everyone in the house was having these experiences at the same time," said one of the daughters. Though nobody ever saw him, the family could hear the cat and feel his presence as he did the things he used to do when he was alive.

Another family member told me TC used to sleep at the end of the bed between her feet. This obviously stopped after the cat died; however, it began again in the two-week period after his death. These strange occurrences continued for approximately one month before he apparently moved on for good. "It was freaky but cool," said the youngest member of the family.

HE LOOKS LIKE A GIANT BAT

While researching and investigating encounters with the entities that I've written about in this book, I visited a friend of mine who is a Catholic priest to say confession and receive a blessing of protection. During our conversation, I told the priest what people were telling me in order to get his reaction. I asked the priest's opinion about these things and whether he thought they were telling the truth.

The priest told me that he believed in such encounters and has had encounters with them as well. I asked him to elaborate. This is his story.

"The devil first appeared to me in a fiery face on two occasions when I was to be ordained into the church. I guess he was trying to discourage me from becoming a priest," my friend said. I asked whether he has had any encounters since that time. "Yes, The devil comes to me at night in my room in the rectory of the church almost every night.

"When I fall asleep I am awakened by the sound of rustling. It wakes me up and I see him standing in the corner of the room."

I asked him, "What does he look like, Father?"

"He looks like a giant bat. Sometimes he lies on my chest so I can't breathe, and on one occasion I got up and he walked toward me and pulled a crucifix off from around my neck and threw it against the wall. I never found it again although I saw it hit the wall. I had to buy a new one."

The priest told me he recites the prayers of exorcism every night before going to sleep but it still comes into the room. As I questioned the priest further, I could see that he was becoming anxious and said, "I don't want to talk about it anymore. This thing is going to make me pay for telling you about this."

It has been quite a while since we spoke to each other even though I have called several times; I think he is afraid to discuss the incidents with me again for fear of retaliation.

SECTION THREE

Unidentified Flying Objects

Ezekiel 1:4 I looked and I saw a windstorm coming out of the north–an immense cloud with flashing lightning and surrounded by brilliant light. The center of the fire looked like glowing metal.

Ezekiel 1:5 and in the fire was what looked like four living creatures. In appearance their form was that of a man.

FOLLOWED BY A UFO

It was a clear cold night in October of 1973. Sandy had just completed an art history term paper for a college course in Kirksville, Missouri. She was returning home to Memphis on Route 136, a hilly, winding road. Visibility was as excellent that night. As Sandy was driving along the road, she happened to glance in the rear view mirror and noticed some lights in the sky. At first she thought it was a helicopter, but after watching the craft a little longer she realized it could not be a helicopter because it was circular and it had blinking lights around the perimeter.

Sandy kept looking back at the craft. There was no traffic on this country road, especially at this time of night. That part of the road was extremely dark, so it was easy to see the craft as it lit up the entire area. Sandy said she remembers being simply fascinated at the thing. She continued to look back at the craft and felt like it was following her car, although she didn't feel scared or threatened at all.

Sandy was so immersed in watching the craft that she lost control of the vehicle. She drove off the road and down a steep embankment. Her head slammed into the rear view mirror, which broke off the windshield and cut her above the right eye. Sandy left the vehicle and ran through a cornfield in the direction of a house she had seen from her car. The occupants took her to the emergency room at a local hospital, where she received eight stitches. Sandy didn't mention her sighting of the craft to the doctor. His only question was, "Were you wearing your seat belt?"

Sandy told me that her experience is just as vivid now as it was 35 years ago. She continues to insist that the operators of the craft where friendly and didn't mean her any harm. She also said, "When I think of it, I feel a little bit special to have seen it."

IT FOLLOWED US THROUGH
THE WOODS

About 15 years ago, two boys about seven and nine years old were riding dirt bikes one afternoon in Wareham, Massachusetts, when they encountered something that still baffles them today. The boys were having a good time riding the dirt bike but had lingered too long, and it was now getting dark very quickly. For safety reasons, they decided to push the bike down a path they considered a short cut to Great Neck Road. Their house was just a short distance from where the shortcut ended at the paved road.

It is unclear who first saw it, but it quickly became apparent to both brothers that a ball of light was coming toward them as they made their way down the winding path. They started walking faster. Neither boy wanted the light to catch up to them, and they were only halfway to the road. At first, the brothers thought that the light might be coming from a person carrying a flashlight trying to get out of the woods themselves. However, it also seemed strange that they had not encountered anyone the entire day they had been in the woods. The brothers kept looking behind them, realizing then that the light was much larger than that of a flashlight. It now appeared to them as a ball of light rather than a beam of light. One brother said he thought it was about 2 feet in diameter. The other one thought it was larger than that.

The brothers realized the light was gaining on them, and they could no longer keep the same distance between them and it. They could see that no one was holding or carrying the ball of light; it was just floating along, above the path about three to four feet above the ground. The floating ball was not traveling in a straight line through the woods but rather following the exact route the boys had taken. When the boys finally reached the road, the ball of light continued toward them. They stopped to watch the light as it reached the end of the path. However, unlike the boys, the light ball didn't stop. Instead, it took a 90-degree turn to the left and took off down the road at tremendous speed. The boys ran the rest of the way home to tell their parents about what had happened to them. Their father dismissed the ball of light as an atmospheric electrical phenomenon known as ball lighting.

UFO OVER BIG SANDY POND

This story was told to me by a man who in the 1980s lived in a small cottage on the water's edge of Sandy Pond in Plymouth, Massachusetts. I was at working in Wareham when James came into the business and announced that he had seen a UFO the previous night hovering over Sandy Pond. James was excited and was sure that what he witnessed was not something man made. Four other people listened incredulously as James told us his story.

"I was woken up by an bright light that lit up the entire inside of my house," James began. "I got up and ran to the living room where the light seemed to be the brightest. The curtain for the picture window was open, and the bright light was emanating from a diamond-shaped UFO hovering a couple yards above the pond. The UFO sparkled a thousand times brighter than a diamond. It literally lit up the entire outdoors.

"I ran into my teenage daughter's room and woke her up so that she could see what I was seeing. She was as dumbfounded as I was at the sight of the UFO lowering a three- to four-inch diameter hose into the pond. I wanted to get my camera and take some pictures, but I was afraid I would miss it taking off. We watched it take off straight up into the sky at tremendous speed."

UFO OVER FENWAY PARK

I interviewed a gentleman who claims to have seen a UFO hovering over Fenway Park in Boston about 15 years ago. The man described a cigar shaped UFO with windows along the sides of the craft. He claimed that he could also distinguish the shapes of the occupants through the windows. The man also stated that there was a baseball game going on in the park at the time, and though he couldn't see the field from his home, he definitely could see the UFO. He didn't think that the people attending the game were aware of the craft because it was way above the glare of the lights. The only way the craft could be seen was from high above the lights looking down at the craft.

UFO ENCOUNTER IN ROCHESTER

In 1972 Mark was nineteen years old, living with his parents while attending a local community college. After class one day, Mark and his college friend Steve decided to go to the movies. Steve was going to ask Mary, a friend of his girlfriend, if she wanted to be Mark's date for the evening. Mary decided to go, and the four went to the movies.

After the movies, the teenagers ate at McDonald's, and the two couples decided to head home for the evening. Because it was still early and they were having a great time together, Mark and Mary decided to go somewhere and talk. Mark thought he would take Mary to one of his favorite spots on Snow's Pond Road in Rochester, Massachusetts, where they could park and look at the water. Mary lived with her parents in Mattapoisett, the next town over, and had a curfew of 10:30 p.m. It was about 8 p.m. when they arrived at the pond, and Mark was confident he'd have her home on time.

Mark pulled his Pinto into a large dirt parking area surrounded by white pine trees about 60 to 70 feet tall. He had been at this spot many times before while visiting his aunt, who had a cottage on the lake. They were sitting in the car enjoying each other's company when Mark had a strange feeling that they were being watched. The couple looked up at the same time to see the tops of the pine trees all lit up. The lights seemed to be rotating very fast in a clockwise motion around the center of what looked to be a dark round cloud. Mary began to panic. Mark rolled down the window of the car, looked up, and saw the dark object with spinning lights hovering about 100 feet above. Mark was beginning to panic himself.

"Holy Shit, let's get out of here!" Mark yelled. As Mary urged him to hurry, he couldn't start the car. He turned the key repeatedly and even removed the key and placed it back in the ignition, but the engine just would not crank over. Mark felt absolutely helpless. It was very dark now, but the lights emanating from the object told them it was still hovering above their vehicle. Mark tried not to let Mary know how scared he really was. As they sat there in the car, Mark made sure the car doors were locked. Whatever the thing was, Mark was certain that it was the reason why the car would not start. Mark noted that the object didn't make any noise at all.

After what seemed like an hour, Mark was finally able to start the car. He heard Mary yell, "Please let's get out of here!" Mark immediately turned on the lights, floored the gas pedal, and drove as fast as he could down the dirt road, racing to reach the paved road and civilization. As he sped down the dirt road he could still see the lights illuminating the treetops. The thing was following them. He thought that if he could get to the houses at the end of the road, they would not be alone. Mark was driving fast now, blowing the horn frantically hoping someone would hear it and come out to investigate. The weird craft would not leave them alone, and it was obvious that it was under intelligent control. The couple continued down the road toward the houses, and the road ahead looked to be better lit than where they had come from. Mark realized the lights emanating from the object were no longer visible and that the object had disappeared.

Mark asked Mary, "Where did the lights go?" The object was no longer pursuing them. She said, "I see it over to the right of us." They reached the houses at the end of the dirt road, hoping to get help or at least tell someone what had just happened, but the houses were in complete darkness. They kept driving until they reached the paved road. Then they noticed a large light in the sky above a pasture to the right of their vehicle. Mark said, "It jumped around in the sky like a popcorn kernel in a popcorn machine." Despite Mary's objections, Mark decided to follow the object. They stopped at the side of the road occasionally to observe the object darting back and forth through the sky. They watched the object as it appeared to slow down, eventually stopping to hover over a cranberry bog.

Mark drove toward the object and pulled into the driveway of a house near the bog. Before he got out, he told Mary, "I am going to get someone else to see this, so people won't think we are crazy." He knocked on the front door, and after a short time the door opened and an elderly woman answered it. He pointed to the object silently hovering above the cranberry bog. She yelled to her husband to come quickly and they all ran out to witness the object moving up and down slowly over the bog. The craft made no noise and illuminated an area of the vines in the bog. The elderly woman said to her husband, "Oh my God Oscar, what is it?" He replied, "I have never seen anything like it in my life." The four of them watched the object for a while before it rose from its position above the cranberry bog to a distance of about two hundred feet, hovered there for a moment, and then took off in a northerly direction at tremendous speed. In seconds it was gone.

Mark said he thanked the elderly couple, told them of the their experience with the object earlier, and left. Mark and Mary talked about their encounter with object while driving home. Mary was very late. When Mark got home, he told his parents what he had seen. His dad asked, "What were you smoking?"

Mark described the incident to his friend Steve, who verified that Mary had told the same story. Mark and Mary never saw each other again, Mark wonders if it was because he brought her home late and her parents would not allow her to see him again. Or, perhaps the experience was too intense for a couple on their first date.

Eyewitness sketch (UFO) hovering above vehicle

Eyewitness sketch (UFO) hovering above cranberry bog

THE ALLAGASH PREMONITIONS

Jim had planned a canoe trip in the Maine wilderness for some time and had convinced his brother-in-law Pat to make the trip with him. Pat had enjoyed the camping experience as a child and, having a family of his own now, he had taken them to family campgrounds, which they enjoyed tremendously. Jim had explained to Pat they would be traversing the Allagash Wilderness Waterway by canoe. The trip would take about a week and would end when they reached a section of the St. John River in Canada.

The pair began the trip with great expectations and excitement and ended with relief on Pat's part. The two arrived on the river late on the first day, and they decided to start down the river in the morning after a good night's sleep. The first day was exciting and uneventful. The second day on the river was fun, and the men camped along the river that night. As they continued down the river and into the heart of the wilderness waterway, they noticed that there weren't many other people on the river.

Nights along the river were filled with sounds of rushing water and large animals crashing through the brush to drink by the water's edge. Sleep came easily because of the physical exhaustion of canoeing for ten to fifteen miles a day, a distance calculated to ensure the trip would not exceed seven days. The farther the men advanced into the wilderness, the less the lights of civilization affected the brilliance of the night sky.

On the morning of the fourth day, Jim began to notice that Pat was not himself. He dismissed it as physical exhaustion caused by days of paddling and sitting in a canoe for hours on end. Jim asked Pat if he was feeling all right because he was not acting himself. Pat said, "I am used to camping in parks with my family and this was more than I expected."

The two men continued down the river and found campsites at which to set up camp late in the afternoons. Steve would start a fire and began the task of cooking supper. Pat wasn't interested in eating breakfast or supper. Instead, Pat would pitch his tent and grab a bag of cookies or snacks and retire to his tent for the night. He told Jim that he wanted to travel as any miles a day as possible so they could get back home. Jim was concerned, and cautioned Pat against traveling on this river hastily because of the lack of communication and resourses.

Jim and Pat were on the river late in the afternoon when a ranger in a small powerboat warned them that heavy rain and thunderstorms were forecast for the afternoon and evening. The forest ranger had been the only person they had seen on the river for days. The maps the two men had been using indicated that they would soon be approaching Round Pond, which is a small but deep pond that the river runs into. The river continues through to a section of the river with rapids and rocks called Round Pond Rips. Because of the threat of thundershowers, the pair set up camp on the edge of the river off of Round Pond.

Just before darkness, a man pulled along the side of the river and asked if we could share the campsite with them due to the weather and the danger of going further down the river in the dark. Jim was excited to talk with someone about the trip because Pat had retired to his tent for the night, just as he had done each night since the second night.

The man told Jim that he was a native of Allagash, Maine. He lived in a cabin in the wilderness with his wife and made a living hunting, fishing and trapping. Jim asked the man whether he had ever heard of or seen unidentified flying objects or strange objects in the sky at night. Jim explained that he had felt like he was being watched, especially at night. The man said he had never heard of unidentified flying objects and certainly had never seen one. The man climbed into his tent for the night. When Pat and Jim woke in the morning the man was gone.

The two men continued canoeing the river for the next day or so until they reached the St. John River on the border of Maine and Canada. The driver of a guide service met them with their vehicle. The men loaded their vehicle and drove back to Cape Cod. Over the years, Jim brought up the trip on several occasions, but Pat had little to say about it.

A couple of years after the canoe trip, Jim saw on TV a reenactment of a canoe trip in the 1970s when four men were taken aboard a UFO in the Allagash while fishing. Jim immediately called Pat to tell him what he saw, but Pat was not particularly interested.

Jim continued to enjoy nature and outdoor sports, such as fishing and hunting. During the 1980s, he returned to the Allagash Wilderness Waterway on one more occasion with three friends he had hunted and fished with over the years. Jim was excited to be going back to the river again. However, the day they were to leave for Maine, Jim began feeling anxious and experiencing feelings of impending doom. When the men arrived at the river that afternoon, two of the friends decided to start down the river right away. Jim wasn't feeling well and stayed behind with his canoeing partner until the next morning.

The four men agreed to meet the somewhere along the river the next day. Jim tried hard to shake the feelings of anxiousness, but they remained with him the entire trip. The trip was uneventful and everyone had a good time. Jim didn't tell anyone about the way he was feeling.

Afterward, Jim continued hunting and fishing, but he began having a difficult time being in the woods in the dark. Since he had been a young boy, Jim had always been comfortable hunting and camping in the woods, but now it terrified him.

On one occasion, Jim was turkey hunting in the western part of the state. He remembers walking across a field before daylight, looking up at the stars, and becoming anxious. He said all he could think about was reaching the woods line where he would take cover and be out of site–from what he didn't know. Jim began hearing stories of people who have been abducted on several occasions, some since they were small children. He heard that once a person is abducted, there was a chance that the abductors could find him or her again.

Some years later, while hunting in another part of Maine, Jim was staying in a small hunting camp with six other hunters when he had another unusual experience with something in the sky. He said, "The cabin was pretty far in the woods and there were no lights inside or outside the cabin. The only light we had was from flashlights or gas powered lanterns. It was raining, and no stars were visible in the sky when everyone retired for the night. I was the last person to fall asleep and it was cold and dark in the cabin. I pulled my sleeping bag over my head and went to sleep. It was about 2 p.m. when I woke up and noticed that the cabin seemed lit up from outside the cabin. The light was shining through a skylight in the roof directly over the cot where I was sleeping.

I was looking at a round ball of light, centered directly in the skylight. It appeared to be looking at me. I was scared, and I didn't know why. I called out to my friends, who were no more than ten feet away in any direction, but no one woke to witness what I was seeing. Feeling like a child, I crawled back into my sleeping bag and pulled it over my head." In the meantime, "I was asking myself what the hell, could this be. It was not the moon, it was too small to be the moon and it was perfectly round as a full moon would be, but it was too small and too close to be the moon. After what seemed like five minutes or so I slowly pulled the sleeping bag down and immediately I noticed that the room was still lit up and the object was still positioned in the center of the skylight.

"Once again, I covered my head with the sleeping bag and tried to figure out what this could be. I remember telling myself that by now the moon would have moved out of view of the skylight and it should not still be there. I continued to stare at the object for some time. I was certain I could see stars in the sky around it. I was trying to determine whether it was still raining, although I could not see whether the skylight was wet. I could not muster the courage to walk outside the cabin to look directly at the object. Finally, I fell asleep. When I woke a couple hours later, the cabin was in complete darkness, just as it had been when I first fell asleep. In the morning I told my friends I wanted them to see the object but I could not wake them."

A few years later, Jim was in his bedroom and woke up from a sound sleep absolutely terrified by an intruder. He said, "It was early in the morning. My wife and I were sleeping when I was woken abruptly by what I thought was someone floating out of one the bedroom windows. I remember seeing a shadow of a small person exiting through the side window very quickly. The image in my head was of a small gray alien. The strangest thing about the incident was that I could see only a small part of the intruder from the side but I knew what his face looked like. I could not tell what he was wearing because it happened so fast. It took about a half hour to slow my heart rate, and eventually my terror subsided. If I go hunting now, I find it difficult to leave my vehicle before daylight even though I am armed. Since the Allagash experience, I don't like sleeping outside, even in a tent. I have tried many times but I cannot make it through the night. I am convinced I have had some contact with something and I have the feeling they know where I am all the time."

SECTION FOUR

Things in People's Closets

IT'S HIM AGAIN!

This story was told to me by a woman who said she witnessed something very strange when she was a little girl in a house her grandfather built. After the death of her grandfather, the woman and her family moved into the house. She believes she was in the third or fourth grade at the time she began seeing the stranger in her room. Her bedroom, which she shared with an older sister, was located upstairs. It was unique because her grandfather had built all of the furniture into the walls of the room. As a result of that design, a dormer ran along the outside of the bedroom.

The woman recalled that repeatedly at night she would wake up and see a man enter the bedroom through a door in the storage space of the dormer wall. She said she never saw his face but that he always wore the same clothes, which she described as a plaid shirt and farmer overalls. She said the man came out of the door to the dormer storage space, walked out the door, picked up a television set, walked across the room, and threw the TV out the window. According to the woman, what happened next was even stranger. The man ran down the stairs and outside the house, caught the television and brought it back into her room. Finally, he put the TV back where it had been, then returned into the closet and closed the door.

To the woman's recollection, the man never looked in her direction, and it seemed that he was unaware of her presence at any time. She said that the built-in bed frame she slept on was smaller than the mattress, and this allowed her to slide herself into the space between the mattress and the wall so that he could not see her at all. The woman claimed that what she witnessed continued for quite some time and on many more occasions. She does not remember when she stopped seeing the man in the plaid shirt and overalls.

As I listened to the woman's story, I could see why she never forgot it. She also said family members still tease her about the man in the plaid shirt and farmer's overalls. However, she said she knows what she saw.

HE CAME RIGHT OUT
OF THE CLOSET

Marty lived with his Mother and father and his younger brother in a condominium complex in Bourne, Massachusetts. About 20 years ago, when he was about 10 years old, he had an encounter with a small boy who came out of Marty's bedroom closet in a room that he slept in alone. Marty recounted that his father was working that night and he was home alone with his mother, older brother, and the family dog when the atmosphere in the apartment seemed to change. Marty remembered his mother becoming so frightened that she called his father at work and asked him to come home.

"The air in the apartment seemed to be filled with electricity and noises began coming from inside the walls," Marty said. He remembers wails filling the apartment. The normally docile dog became agitated and started clawing at the carpet in the corner of the living room. Marty remembers that these experiences continued for some time, and only when things stopped did he and his brother go back to bed.

Marty recalled that he had left his night light on that night after the unnerving events of the evening. Just before he dozed off, he saw his closet door open and a small boy emerge from the darkness of the closet. According to Marty, the boy walked to the edge of the bed and sat down on the floor.

"He had on old-fashioned pajamas with the button flap at the back. He also had a pencil and a piece of paper in his hand. I asked him what he was doing. He said, 'I am going to draw you a picture of a farm.'" Marty told me he watched the little boy draw for a while until he got up, went over to him, gave Marty a hug, and disappeared, taking the picture and pencil with him.

The family still speaks of the events of that evening. "I will never forget that little boy," Marty said. The next day the family's neighbors asked about the strange noises they heard coming from Marty's family's apartment that night. The family still wonders what it was that took over their residence that night but whatever it was, the neighbors heard it too.

THE THING AT THE EDGE OF THE BED

It was 1974. We can't say whether the entity that David encountered came out of his closet, but that fact is the thing was in David's room and when it woke him up, it was kneeling at the side of his bed, staring at him, just inches from his face.

David was 10 years old and living with his mother, sister, and older brother in Acushnet, Massachusetts in a small two-story home, which before the incident was free of anything unusual. It was late at night and everyone in the house, including David, was sleeping.

"Something woke me up!" David said. "I had a feeling that someone or something was in the room with me. I opened my eyes to see a small hooded figure kneeling down, staring at me. There was enough light in the room to see that the figure was small had to be kneeling, because its head was just visible over the edge of the bed.

"At first I thought I was dreaming, and I pulled the blankets over my head. I waited for a few seconds before I got up the courage to look at him again. I pulled the covers down slowly, and he was still there. I could make two large eyes, but no other features were visible."

"I don't ever remember being as scared as I was at that moment. I knew I had to get help. I was afraid to scream and I thought for some reason that if I did the thing would do something to me. I lay there for a few more seconds praying that he would just go away and leave me alone. All I could think about now was to run as fast I could and try to get away. I wanted so badly to get downstairs and get help from my mother and brother.

"I was beginning to panic and I was having a hard time catching my breath. Screaming now, in one swift motion I pulled the covers down and jumped out of bed. As both feet hit the floor, I started running out of the room. As I did, the hooded figure that was at the side of my bed a couple seconds ago was now shuffling backward very quickly. In seconds, he backed himself into the corner of the room near the door that was to be my escape route. The way he moved backward and the speed in which he moved without taking his eyes off me was absolutely horrifying.

"Once in the corner the thing seemed to huddle down, draw his shoulders to closer to his body, and bow his head as if to make himself look smaller. This may sound funny but he seemed surprised by my reaction and immediately acted as If he didn't want me to see him anymore. I started running toward the door even though the thing was now huddled only a couple feet away from that door. I was thankful he didn't grab me as I ran by him.

"I threw myself over the rail and landed halfway down the stairs, got up, and ran to my mother's room. I told her what I had seen. She and my brother searched the entire house but they could not find anything. I never saw the hooded figure again. I was hurting for a while from the fall down the stairs. I was lucky I wasn't seriously injured, because the fall from the rail I had jumped over was about eight to ten feet."

"I didn't sleep in that room again for quite a while but when I got older I began sleeping there again---but never when I was alone in the house."

SECTION FIVE

Bigfoot Encounters

BIGFOOT CASE NO. 1

This encounter took place approximately 25 years ago. A couple was traveling along Route 151 in Mashpee, Massachusetts. It was about 2 in the morning. Kate was driving the vehicle, while Mike was a passenger in her car. As the car traveled in a southerly direction, Mike thought he saw something out of the corner of his eye on the opposite shoulder of the road. He asked Kate to turn around, which she did. Mike was not sure of what he had seen but wanted a second look.

As Kate approached the shoulder, Mike realized what he thought he saw was no longer there. Kate then pulled a U-turn near the Nickelodeon Cinema and was once again heading south on route 151. Mike told her to pull into the next road, which she described as an island in the road. Kate said that as she made the turn and was about parallel to the tip of the island, she saw a black Labrador retriever run in front of her car as if it was being chased.

It was then both Kate and Mike saw what they described as an eight-foot human-like creature with dark hair and large eyes, its arms in the air, screaming and running toward the vehicle. Kate said that as the creature approached the vehicle on the passenger side where Mike was sitting, "Mike yelled at the top of his lungs to get moving, Hurry, go!" Kate said she was so frightened that she couldn't operate the vehicle, an older model Toyota with a standard transmission.

Eventually, Kate somehow drove the vehicle back on to Route 151, both of them were traumatized. During the interview, Kate described the creature as extremely agitated for interrupting whatever he was doing at the time.

After hearing Kate's story, I concluded that the creature's intention was to attack the dog. I asked Kate what was going through her mind when she spotted the creature. She said the only words that came to her mind were *missing link*. She said she had never heard the term **Bigfoot**.

Kate added, "Remembering the events of that night still leaves me in disbelief, especially the size of the creature. He was not only at least eight feet tall, but everything about the creature was huge. To say he was barrel chested would be an understatement."

Kate also said that Mike never talked about their experience in Mashpee after that night, not even to her. Kate has since moved to a new address on the Cape. Strangely enough about two years ago a five-foot Bigfoot was spotted on her street eating t of a garbage can.

BIGFOOT CASE NO. 2

This was a sighting rather than an encounter with a large creature in the summer of 1988. The story was told to me by a gentleman named Joe who lived with his family in a home on Plymouth Street in Middleborough, Massachusetts. Joe told me he was pulling out of his driveway, onto Plymouth Street. He noticed that something was out of place on the left side of the road.

Joe said "When you live somewhere for most of your life, you know where every tree and bush is, and that day, something looked different. I noticed a large hairy creature walking briskly down the power line easement toward the paved road. He crossed the road from one side of the easement to the other."

The topography on the left side of the road was relatively flat but there was a steep incline on the right side that the creature negotiated easily before disappearing from my view. The creature resembled what some people have described as Bigfoot and was approximately one hundred yards away when Joe saw it.

Joe said, "The color of the creature's hair was brown and red with streaks of black. Its hair seemed matted on the creature's body. It didn't seem to notice me or my vehicle and didn't seem to be in a hurry. I didn't see the creatures face and he didn't look around but seemed to be focused on getting across the road."

Joe said the experience startled him. He quickly drove to the last place he saw the creature but it had vanished. Joe did walk around at the side of the road, and after finding a very large footprint, he immediately phoned his brother, who met him at the site. I interviewed Joe's brother who, stated that the tracks were clearly defined. Both men tried to impress their own tracks into the soil near the creature's tracks but were unsuccessful. I concluded that whatever had made the impression on the ground had to be much heavier than both men. "The footprint measured well over twelve inches," Joe stated.

No plaster casts were made of the footprint and no photographs were taken. Joe did say that seeing a creature like that\so close to his house made him uncomfortable for a long time. I asked Joe if he ever told anybody what he saw that day. He replied, "Absolutely not. People would think I was crazy."

Bigfoot spotted crossing road on power line

Bigfoot tracks found on right shoulder of road

FOOTPRINT IN THE ROCK

D
an worked as a surveyor during the seventies for a local Cape Cod engineering company when the area was still moderately populated and there were large tracts of land yet to be developed. Some surveys and the property lines established were based on research of old deeds recorded during the 1600s. They were mostly large tracts of woodland, which at one time were farms bounded by stonewalls and piles to indicate corners. The surveyors would sometimes remove stones on a wall to find a small drill hole or a mark scratched on a base rock to indicate a deed written a couple of centuries ago. The base rocks were generally much larger than the rocks above them on the wall.

One day while trying to find a drill hole in a base rock, Thomas, the survey crew chief, told the rest of the crew a story about finding a large footprint in a very large base rock at the bottom of a wall in Sandwich, Massachusetts, about fifteen years prior.

Thomas said, "We were removing the smallest rocks from the wall and as we got down to the base we noticed an impression on the rock. After brushing the dirt and leaves away, we were startled to see a footprint which resembled a human foot but was much larger and much wider than the footprint of a man."

Thomas discussed the curious footprint with the rest of the crew and they all thought that they should contact a local archeologist to inspect the rock and perhaps take it to a museum for display.

The rock was to big and heavy to remove, so the men finished surveying the property and went back to the office. Time passed and they soon the surveyors forgot about the strange footprint in the rock, not having ever called anyone to take photos or investigate. Dan and the rest of the crew did convince Thomas to take them to the place where they had found the rock, but despite numerous attempts, they could not. Thomas tried hard to remember whether he had told anyone who would have removed it but it had been so long and too many property line surveys ago to remember.

Dan said "It was the sixties when they discovered the rock with the footprint, back then nobody carried cameras around with them. However, if it was today we would at least have taken pictures with our cell phones."

It is interesting that the name *Bigfoot* was coined long after Dan found the giant footprint in the rock.

I found Angels to Aliens to be a great collection of firsthand accounts. The author made a very enjoyable and easily readable selection from the vast number of accounts that had been given to him. Countless times I was struck by the common threads to many of the cases in his collection that are also found in the literature of each topic. His work drives home the point that if you just take time to simply and politely ask, many will tell you their story. As the reader goes through these stories, many will hear much of the thoughts and feelings of those whom had these strange happenings, and most will relate to them. This is more than just a mere collection of "Campfire Ghost Stories", as it brings home the human element and personal connection that cannot be shared by a second hand telling. The reader will be thrilled, humbled and amazed by the courage by the courage and bravery that each of the storytellers bring to life with their accounts of experiencing the unexplained. I have read and actually been in many parts of many books of all aspects of the unexplained in my many decades of my work in the field, but I can say that this book is well worth the time to invest in reading if you like to hear it from the horse's mouth.

-Matthew Moniz

ABOUT THE AUTHOR

R obert Ethier began his quest to document encounters with paranormal entities in 2007, but his interest really began much earlier. Within two weeks of moving into a new home on Cape Cod in the late 1970s, his family began to be harassed by an unseen entity that was determined to drive them out of the house. That story is documented in this book as "There Is Someone or Something in This House Besides Us."

Previously employed as a land surveyor and environmental specialist for thirty-five years, Robert currently works in municipal public health in Massachusetts.

Printed in the United States
By Bookmasters